Damian M

LIBEL LAW: A JOURN

Damian McHugh
Barrister-at-Law

Libel Law

A JOURNALIST'S HANDBOOK

WITH A FOREWORD BY
Hugh J. O'Flaherty, SC

THE ROUND HALL PRESS

The typesetting of this book was
produced by Gilbert Gough Typesetting, Dublin
for The Round Hall Press Limited
Kill Lane, Blackrock, Co. Dublin.

© Damian McHugh 1989

BRITISH LIBRARY CATALOGUING IN PUBLICATION DATA
Libel law: a journalist's handbook.
1. Ireland. (Republic). Defamation. Law
344.17063'4

ISBN 0-947686-55-X

ACKNOWLEDGMENTS
The text of the Defamation Act, 1961 is
reproduced with the permission of the
Controller, Stationery Office, Dublin.

Printed in Great Britain by BPCC Wheatons Ltd, Exeter

To my wife, Claire, and to our children,
Damian Jnr., Trudi, Avril, Debbie, Robert and Shane

Contents

	FOREWORD	9
	PREFACE	11
1	LIBEL	13
	Truth and libel	14
	The essence of libel: defamation	14
	Publication	14
	Criminal libel	15
	Guidelines	16
	The test	17
	Perils	20
	Libels on corporate bodies	21
2	DEFENDING A LIBEL ACTION	22
	The memo	23
	Publishing an apology	23
	The source of the libel	25
	Notebooks	26
	The defendants: who may be sued?	26
	The case for the defence	27
	Report versus comment	29
	Fair comment	30
	The public's right to be heard	30
3	COURT REPORTING	31
	A hearing in chambers	33

	A hearing in the Judge's home	33
	When is a private hearing not private?	34
	The Constitution	35
	Reports of judicial proceedings	36
	The hearing	37
	The report	38
	The 'pick-up'	39
	Names and addresses	39
	Third parties	40
	Headings	41
	District Court preliminary examainations	41
4	CONTEMPT OF COURT	42
	Definition	42
	Press photographers and contempt	45
	Scandalizing the court	46
	Comment by newspapers on court proceedings	46
	Sub judice: limits on publication	47
	The Constitutional guarantee of freedom of expression	48
5	PRIVACY	50
	Trespass	50
	Nuisance	50
	Breach of confidence	51
	The right to be left alone	54
6	OTHER TOPICS	55
	Copyright	55
	The Official Secrets Act, 1963	55
	Section 31	57
	Book publishers	59
7	THE NATIONAL UNION OF JOURNALISTS	60
	APPENDIX 1: The Defamation Act, 1961	63
	APPENDIX 2: A guide to legal terms	77

Foreword

Damian McHugh has served a long apprenticeship in journalism. In particular he became a very experienced court reporter. Then he studied for the Bar and was duly called. There has always been a close affinity between the professions of law and journalism in this country. Many legal aspirants did radio and newspaper work and the virtue of conciseness — so essential in both spheres — was learned.

Now Damian has put his experience in both disciplines to good use by producing this excellent work. He sets out to explain the law for the journalist and he does so in a simple, direct style. I am glad that he has kept the language of the newsroom and the caseroom to the fore.

Readers will find reference to many cases which cannot be found in any of the official reports. I was astonished at the accuracy of his recall of cases going back as long ago as twenty years. Therefore, his hints for court reporters are particularly good. There is a fine tradition of court reporting in this country. Journalists do strive to present both sides of a case fairly. After all, the Constitution says that it is *justice* that is to be rendered in public — not law or rhetoric. Just as a good newspaper has been defined as like a nation talking to itself, so it is the duty and task of the journalist to reflect this in the accuracy of his reporting.

The task of getting everything right — and any copy has to go through many hands — is not an easy one. There is no magic formula by which trouble will be avoided. Even a judge of over forty years standing (in the neighbouring jurisdiction) when he came to write a book of memoirs and criticisms was threatened with a libel writ and went through much anguish.

While no one can guarantee immunity this book will certainly help stave off proceedings. We are certainly a litigious people and getting more so. The Oireachtas rather mysteriously has retained jury trials in defamation actions, yet not for litigants who may have sustained appalling physical injuries.

Aside from dealing with libel, there are useful chapters on contempt of court, privacy and related matters. There is a glossary on legal terms.

I am honoured to commend this book to all who are interested in the interaction of the law with the media.

For the working, and often harassed, journalist I would say: always have this book at hand. As a journeyman barrister I will, myself, be sure to keep it at hand.

Hugh J. O'Flaherty, SC
Law Library, Four Courts, Dublin

Preface

This manual has been given life as a result of an advice given by Professor Kevin Boyle of Essex University and Marie McGonagle, lecturer in the Department of Law, University College, Galway in their jointly produced work *A Report on Press Freedom and Libel* commissioned by the national newspapers of Ireland, in which they suggested that journalists in Ireland should have a handbook available to them acquainting them of the libel laws. In the short period that has elapsed since publication of their report, I have endeavoured to compile a manual designed to be of everyday use to the practical journalist, to students of journalism and to those involved in the various aspects of communications whose work brings them into touch with the public and the dissemination of information touching on the lives and fortunes of a great many people.

This handbook does not claim to be an exhaustive text on the law governing the Press and the media in general nor does it purport to offer any suggestions which might lead to a reform of the law of defamation. That is a matter within the province of the Law Reform Commission following a reference by the Attorney General, Mr John L. Murray, SC. Neither does this publication claim to be exhaustive in terms of the various topics dealt with. In possible future editions I would hope to expand on topics covered in this handbook in addition to extending the range of the legal microscope for the benefit of the practical newspaper person. In facing up to the task offered to me at Christmas by Bart Daly, Editor of *Irish Law Reports Monthly*, I have had to wear two hats or, to be more precise, a wig and a hat. What follows in the handbook may not save legal costs once a serious error has been made, but it may reduce or avoid such a bill and damages if the general guidelines and advices are observed. This handbook will have achieved its objective if journalists, from the rawest cub reporter to those with heaviest editorial responsibility, can condition their respective minds to be being merely suspicious when dealing with what might appear to be defamatory material. If the warning bell sounds automatically as a result of elementary legal knowledge, the journalist will have done his profession proud and may have saved his employer untold financial consequences. Francis Bacon's immortalised words are appropriate: 'If a man will begin with certainties, he shall end in doubts; but if he will be content to begin with doubts, he shall end in certainties.' It only needs to be added that prevention is better than cure. The following pages have been prepared without recourse to excessive legal language, without reference to the titles of cases and, in particular, without identifying the Irish newspapers involved in the libel and contempt proceedings adverted to. Suffice to try and learn by the experience.

It would be remiss of me not to make special mention of Bart Daly and Michael Adams, Directors of The Round Hall Press Ltd for their encouragement, to Mel Christle, BL for his helpful advice, to Thomas McCann, librarian, for research help and to Hugh O'Flaherty, SC, not alone for writing the Foreword, but for his invaluable help in getting the finished product to print.

There has always been a need for a work such as this, never more so than at present. If this small contribution goes some way towards meeting that need, the effort will have been worthwhile.

Damian McHugh
1 February 1989

1

Libel

Libel is the legal name for defamatory words written, printed, or otherwise permanently represented (such as in a painting or effigy). *Slander* is the term applied to defamatory words uttered by word of mouth, i.e. the spoken word. Journalists are therefore concerned not so much with slander as with libel; this applies as much to broadcasting journalists as it does to those working in the printing media.

The tort (i.e a civil wrong or legal wrong) of *defamation* protects interests in reputation. It consists in the publication to a third person of matter 'containing an untrue imputation against the reputation of another' (*Gatley on Libel and Slander*). One classic definition was provided by the Irish courts in 1971 which has been followed ever since. According to it defamation is the wrongful publication of a false statement about a person, which tends to lower that person in the eyes of right-thinking members of society or tends to hold that person up to hatred, ridicule or contempt, or causes that person to be shunned or avoided by right-thinking members of society.

It is of vital importance, therefore, that journalists should understand what is and what is not defamatory, or in other words, what constitutes an actionable libel. Newspapers, magazines, radio and television do not as a rule knowingly publish defamatory words; but pure inadvertence may easily result in a libel suit and heavy damages, as many publications have found to their cost in court—not to mention the substantial sums handed over to plaintiffs in settlements reached before their actions even come on for trial.

TRUTH AND LIBEL

Libel is not a question of truth and falsehood. The old adage 'The greater the truth the greater the libel' holds good. In certain cases the truth of libellous matter, if it can be proved to the satisfaction of a court, may relieve the defendants from legal liability; but such justification is entirely a question of evidence and may be very difficult and costly to establish. The journalist, whether reporter, sub-editor or editor, who OKs a libel because he or she believes in the truth of the matter, is asking for trouble.

The important thing for a journalist to learn is how to recognize a libel.

THE ESSENCE OF LIBEL: DEFAMATION

No matter what time is left to the deadline for copy, the question which the journalist must ask in every situation is: 'Are these words capable of a defamatory meaning?' The journalist who suspects, deep down, that there may be a problem but says nothing and, instead, allows the copy through to the printers or permits the recorded tape to be broadcast or screened, is acting irresponsibly. If the question does arise, it is far better that it be decided or, at the very least, be discussed and brought to the attention of a superior prior to publication than later by a court with damages and costs the ultimate sanction. The golden rule should be implanted in the mind of every journalist: *When in doubt, leave out.* But the journalist who will take the trouble to attend to some elementary principles need seldom be in doubt and once he or she understands these principles, perhaps the most important rule is: *Read or even re-read the copy before handing it in.*

PUBLICATION

Since reputation is one's estimation in the eyes of others, no defamation can occur without publication. Pride, self-respect and dignity may be affronted by a communication to the person defamed, but without publication to a third person there is no hurt to reputation and, therefore, no wrong of defamation. This distinguishes *the tort of defamation* from *criminal libel*, for which there may be a prosecution without proof of publication to a third person. There is an amelioration for persons who are in the final stage of the distribution process of a libel for example, newspaper vendors, newsagents and booksellers. Some cases decided over the years by the courts, both here and in Britain, have provided leniency in the rule regarding publication. If, as persons carrying on their business properly, they neither knew nor ought to have known that the newspaper or book contained a libel, they are not deemed to be publishers.

Television is clearly included as a method of publication because section 14(2) of the Defamation Act, 1961 provides:

> Any reference in this Part (i.e. Part III) to words shall be construed as including a reference to visual images, gestures and other methods of signifying meaning.

Broadcasting is also covered. To put the matter beyond doubt, section 15 of the Act of 1961 states:

> For the purposes of the law of libel and slander the broadcasting of words by means of wireless telegraphy shall be treated as publication in permanent form.

CRIMINAL LIBEL

Apart from civil defamation, newspapers are at risk of being prosecuted on a criminal charge for publishing a defamatory libel. Criminal proceedings for libel can be brought by private as well as by public prosecutors, but no criminal prosecution can be commenced against any proprietor, publisher, editor or any person responsible for the publication of a newspaper or any libel published, without an order being obtained first from a judge of the High Court sitting *in camera*. Section 8 of the Defamation Act ensures that notice of the application is given to the person accused, who has the right to be heard before leave is granted. The 1961 Act provides for the charge to be tried on indictment by a judge and jury, but the Act also provides circumstances where it may be tried summarily by the District Court, with provision for imposing fines and/or prison sentences on conviction on indictment and a fine only on summary conviction.

Not every libel could result in the newspapers being tried on a criminal prosecution. The essence of libel as a criminal offence is that it tended to provoke a breach of the peace.

GUIDELINES

There are four classes of comment which are always highly dangerous because they give a plaintiff a good right of action. Only the strictest proof of their truth, which may easily be impossible, will save the defendants from heavy damages. These kinds of comment are:

(1) words which impute unchastity or adultery to any woman or girl;

(2) words affecting a person's official, professional or business reputation;

(3) words imputing a criminal offence punishable by death or imprisonment;

(4) words imputing a contagious disease which tends to exclude the sufferer from society.

Regarding (1) above, it would seem reasonable to include men and boys in this class, although they are not mentioned in the Defamation Act, 1961 from which (1) and (2) are taken.

The mere utterance of such aspersions by word of mouth is an actionable slander; in writing or print or through broadcast they are a far more serious matter. The mere hint of such criticism should be enough to set off the alarm signals in the vigilant journalist.

The journalist's motive and intention matters little. It will not help the defendant on the day of trial to plead that he acted as the guardian of public morality or as the protector of the wronged. It is just possible that in awarding damages a jury may pay some attention to the motive actuating the publication of the libel. But the jury may not, and it is, therefore, unsafe to bank on the possibility.

Neither will it help the defendant to plead that he was the victim of an honest mistake or that he was misinformed. 'It is the duty of a newspaper to test the truth of its information. Mistake is no defence; inadvertence no excuse', Charles Pilley, barrister-at-law, wrote more than fifty years ago, in his excellent book *Law for Journalists*. Such classes of comment, therefore, should be avoided at all costs. So also should many others, less usual, which we need not go into here.

THE TEST

Knowing or identifying matter which is defamatory is not easy, and it is particularly difficult to bring a clear mind to the issue when working to deadlines. When the journalist out in the field or the colleague 'knocking out a story' with the news editor pressing for copy, has his or her mind solely directed to producing the copy, the reality is that libel and lurking dangers are far from his or her mind.

However, the test of what is defamatory is the objective 'reasonable person' test. Except in the small number of cases which are tried in the Circuit Court — where a judge sitting alone decides the action — the 'reasonable person' is a High Court jury. The jury, with guidance from the judge, will decide that issue and also the amount of damages which the plaintiff should be awarded.

Since the tort of defamation both limits freedom of speech and intrudes on the freedom of the Press, certain safeguards have been built into the legal requirements. One of these is trial by jury, a principle recognized by the Courts Act, 1988 which abolished the presence of juries in High Court personal injury actions but retained juries for trying libel actions.

It should be noted that what was regarded by a jury as defamatory fifty years ago would not necessarily hold good in 1989. What might have been public feeling even ten years ago, might not necessarily be public feeling now.

So, just to re-cap, the essential ingredients of defamation are:
• The words must refer to the plaintiff.

- The words must be published to a third party.
- The words must be defamatory or capable of being defamatory.

Hatred, ridicule and contempt The Civil Bill (the originating document in a Circuit Court action) or the Statement of Claim served by the plaintiff on the defendant in a High Court action for libel or an Affidavit grounding an application for an injunction to stop the publication of an allegedly defamatory matter will contain a paragraph something like the following:

> As a result of the said publication, the plaintiff has been greatly injured in his credit and reputation and in his office as aforesaid and has been brought into public odium, hatred, ridicule and contempt.

The wording of the legal document will depend on the circumstances of the particular case but certainly the words 'hatred', 'ridicule' and 'contempt' will be included in all cases of libel by the barrister drafting the document. On the face of it, the definition is an extremely wide one, giving a plaintiff latitude to issue a writ for libel if an unkind word is published against him or her. However, for the comfort of the harassed journalist, the law allows considerable latitude of comment to the Press, as will become apparent when we consider the various defences open to the publisher of a libel.

An elementary knowledge of the law of libel will enable the editor to gauge the risk he is taking, and, if he must sail close to the wind, to trim his sails with prudence. The Irish are an extremely litigious race and, with such heavy, indeed swingeing, damages being awarded in courts of late, the days of 'Publish and be damned' are clearly numbered.

Examples of libel There are no fixed rules as to what constitutes defamation. Much depends on the circumstances of each case, but it may be helpful to consider certain examples of what has actually been held libellous by the Irish courts, if only to indicate the way in which these matters strike the judicial mind.

Bryan M.E. McMahon and William Binchy in their book *Irish Law of Torts* chronicle some useful examples:

• A suggestion made by an auctioneer that the plaintiff had not acted in accordance with the high traditions of his profession as a solicitor was accepted as being defamatory.

• To say of a well-known professional footballer that he never used his right foot in kicking the ball because he was unable to do so was capable of being defamatory if it was not true.

• Imputations of sexual impropriety made against the plaintiffs in a book were held to be defamatory.

• To impute that the plaintiff made deliberate false statements to a local corporation for the purpose of deceiving the corporation, and that the plaintiff was unfit for public office was also held to be defamatory.

• To accuse a person wrongfully of theft is defamatory.

• In England, it has been held libellous and actionable to say of a man that he is insane.

• It was held libellous and actionable to say that a man was a bigot in religious matters.

However, it was held not libellous of a layman that he 'knows no law' but to say it of a lawyer would be highly defamatory as reflecting upon him in his profession.

Vulgar abuse Vulgar abuse is defined as the reviling of a person in terms which are common, crude, uncouth, rude, coarse or in bad taste. It has always been accepted that vulgar abuse of a person is not defamatory but, while this is largely true, no such rule exists and journalists should be wary in the extreme.

Malice Malice is not an essential element of a libel. Even where there has been an absence of ill-will or spite or of libellous intention, damages may be awarded. The most innocent-looking words may be held defamatory if they fail the 'reasonable person' test in the minds of the jurors in the High Court or the judge alone in the Circuit Court.

PERILS

Generally, any words which reflect on the plaintiff's moral, intellectual or professional character are libellous and may give rise to grounds for an action in damages. As with every individual action commenced at law, each case must be judged on its own merits.

Indirect libel — innuendo It is not only by direct statement that a libel may be conveyed. An apparent innocent remark may be held to be defamatory because of a hidden meaning which the words carry. Where the words complained of are *prima facie* innocent, the plaintiff must prove that the words have a secondary meaning which makes them defamatory.

One of the best examples is to be found in a case involving Daily Mirror Newspapers about sixty years ago where they published a photograph of a Mr Cassidy (otherwise known as Corrigan) with a Miss X and stated, innocently, that their engagement had been announced. At the time, the plaintiff, Mrs Mildred Cassidy, and her husband did not live together but he occasionally stayed with her at her flat. The caption with the photograph stated: 'Mr M. Corrigan, the race horse owner, and Miss X, whose engagement has been announced'.

Mrs Cassidy alleged that she had suffered damage through the publication insomuch as it was intended, and by several people understood, to mean that K.E. Cassidy was not her husband but was living with her in immoral cohabitation.

The jury in England held that Mrs Cassidy had been libelled and awarded her £500. The Court of Appeal held that the publication was capable of conveying a defamatory meaning of Mrs Cassidy and dismissed the appeal taken by the newspaper.

Lord Justice Russell said in the course of his judgment: 'Liability for libel does not depend on the intention of the defamer, but on the fact of defamation. If you once reach the conclusion that the published matter in the present case amounts to or involves a statement that Mr Corrigan is an unmarried man, then, in my opinion, those persons who knew the circumstances might reasonably consider the statement defamatory of the plaintiff.'

Libel without mentioning names The case also provides a good example of how a newspaper or any organ of publication, including radio or television, can libel an individual in such a way as to give him or her a good cause of action without actually mentioning the name. If the words can reasonably be understood to refer to the plaintiff, damages may be recovered.

Photographers The case also produced a result which serves as a warning to photographers, as well as to writing journalists, not to always accept things for what they seem. Libel can lurk in the caption to a photograph just as much as it can anywhere else in the newspaper columns.

LIBELS ON CORPORATE BODIES

Corporate bodies may defend their good name in court. The libel must reflect on the conduct of the corporation as such, not just on the individuals composing it.

In a general way, newspapers, magazines and current affairs programmes on radio and TV are free to criticize public bodies and, unless corruption is alleged, there is no great risk of a libel action being taken.

Similarly, provided no corrupt motive is alleged, the decisions of judges and the behaviour of the Gardaí and other public officials may be criticized. But as regards judges and the courts, prudence must be observed for fear of the contempt laws (see Chapter 4).

2

Defending a libel action

A writ for libel is rarely issued without an initial contact between the plaintiff or the plaintiff's solicitor and the newspaper. The vast majority of disputes are settled out of court during the course of preliminary negotiations between the parties. By and large, initial contact is made by way of a solicitor's letter to the proprietors, and usually to the editor as well, drawing attention to the alleged libel and demanding a retraction or apology and an offer of amends which usually means compensation in damages.

Consideration must then be given to the question whether it would be more prudent to retreat into the position of offering the apology and a cash payment to cover agreed damages and costs, or to fight. Delay in making a decision at this stage may prove very expensive later, as many publishers have found. Depending on the exact circumstances of the case, the publisher might be left with no alternative but to allow the matter to proceed to court, ignoring the request for an apology and so on, because, if nothing else, it may be considered that the plaintiff is 'chancing his arm' in the hope of making some 'soft' money; but in other cases where, for instance, mistake has arisen through carelessness or inadvertence at some stage in the reporting or printing process, or where information in good faith has been shown to be erroneous, it would be foolish to risk a court action in the slight hope that it will turn out alright on the day.

THE MEMO

After a quick check by the editor, usually with the relevant news editor, regarding the substance of the complaint, it is usually left to the news editor to establish the *bona fides* of the complaint. If it appears that the alleged libel originated in the work of a journalist, the individual concerned will be asked to write a memorandum setting out in detail what happened on the particular occasion.

PUBLISHING AN APOLOGY

When the dust settles after the initial investigation and it transpires that there was some substance to the complaint resulting in some wrong — no matter to what degree — the question which must be addressed is whether an apology or correction should be published. While the publisher may wish to exercise his prerogative and not offer an apology, experience has shown that there is little to be gained from adopting that stand. If a member of the public has been defamed, it is only right and just that that person's character should be vindicated as soon as possible after the damage was caused. Should the publisher fail to publish an apology or delay in doing so until the die is well and truly cast on the sea of litigation, almost certainly the award of damages will be greater than it otherwise would be. Recently one Dublin daily designated space on a particular page for the sole purpose of offering apologies and clarifications, a practice which would commend itself in mitigation should any of the matters affected reach court. There is always the possibility also that promptness in publishing an apology or clarification will sway those affected from issuing proceedings, and the lead given by that newspaper could usefully be followed by all.

Section 17 of the Defamation Act deals with the question of apologies:

> In any action for defamation, it shall be lawful for the defendant (after notice in writing of his intention so to do, duly given to the plaintiff at the time of filing or delivering the plea in the action)

to give evidence, in mitigation of damage, that he made or offered an apology to the plaintiff for such defamation before the commencement of the action, or as soon afterwards as he had an opportunity of doing so, in case the action shall have been commenced before there was an opportunity of making or offering such apology.

This is saying, in effect, that the defendant may give evidence to the court that he offered an apology to the defendant before the proceedings were commenced or as soon as he had an opportunity to do so. The legislation clearly recognizes that this evidence may be given in order to reduce the damages against the defendant. By failing to give the apology, the defendant is not helping his own cause and by delaying in publishing an apology he is aggravating the libel to an extent that may be used by the plaintiff to receive even greater damages later.

Whatever the rights or wrongs of the alleged libellous matter of which complaint is made, section 17 puts the newspaper, magazine, broadcasting station or whatever publisher is involved into a Catch 22 situation. If an apology is published in the first instance, guilt is being declared at a very early stage and the only matter remaining is the amount of compensation that the plaintiff should recover. However, if the apology is not published or is delayed, the legislation is there to be used against the publisher at the hearing.

Publishers are placed in a similar dilemma by the Rules of the Superior Courts which provide at Order 22: 'In actions for libel or slander . . . money may not be paid into Court under this rule unless liability is admitted in the defence.' This provision, which is confined to defamation actions, effectively precludes publishers from lodging money in court unless the publisher is admitting fault. One consequence of this is that the defendant is denied the relief available to every other defendant litigant in tort action of not having to pay the major proprotion of the legal costs if the eventual award of damages by the judge or jury fails to exceed the amount lodged in court by the defendant.

Before departing from this topic, reference must be made to section 21 of the 1961 Act which provides that a person who unintentionally defames another person may make an offer of amends, including the publication of a suitable correction of the words complained of and 'a sufficient apology'. If the offer is accepted and is duly performed, no proceedings shall be taken against the person making the offer in respect of the publication in question. But if the offer is not accepted, then the publisher/defendant may use the evidence of the offer and the fact that the matter was published innocently by him as a defence. However, in order to avail of this defence, the publisher must, among other things, be able to prove that he exercised all reasonable care in relation to the publication.

THE SOURCE OF THE LIBEL

Other journalists involved in processing the particular copy may also be asked to write memos. Usually, the personnel concerned will be working from memory in detailing accounts of what transpired as they handled the copy at successive stages. While it will normally become apparent early in the investigation where the problem arose, all too often it emerges that it originated with the journalist in the first instance 'taking a chance' that the story was OK or through inadvertence or, indeed, through 'picking-up' a story from a colleague. But not always. Fortunes have been handed away in damages through a sub-editor's carelessness when reducing or re-writing the submitted copy — through bad punctuation and writing up misleading headings.

The history of libel actions has also taught journalists and newspaper lawyers that the case room has been a fertile source of grounds for action. A word, a sentence or a paragraph dropped from a story can drastically alter the original story to create a dangerous imbalance. One working journalist, so sensitive to the word 'now' appearing as 'not' in the newspapers he works for, recently resolved never to write the word 'now' in his copy because of the frequency with which the error appeared without being spotted by the proof readers.

NOTEBOOKS

Newspapers and other publications would be well advised to issue reporting staff with notebooks — as at least one Dublin daily does — with an instruction that they be retained, duly dated, for up to twelve months. Freelance journalists employed on a docket basis could be similarly instructed. If such a course were adopted and checked from time to time to see that it was being observed, the task of proprietors, editors and those charged with checking complaints would be simplified.

The one disadvantage of retaining notebooks is that they would form part of the material that would be handed to the plaintiff's side prior to the hearing should they be granted an order of discovery by the court since the notes were prepared in the first instance when the libel proceedings were not in contemplation. Nevertheless, the advantages considerably outweigh the disadvantages in practical terms and, on balance, notebooks should be kept.

THE DEFENDANTS: WHO MAY BE SUED?

Every person who is concerned in the publication complained of may be named as a defendant in a libel action. These would include:

- The newspaper owners or, in the case of Radio Teleffs Éireann, the RTE Authority
- The editor
- Publishers
- The reporter
- Printers
- Wholesale distributors.

In most cases only the owners and the editor and, possibly the reporter — if there is a bye-line on the story — are joined, but sometimes the editor is left out and only the owners are named as the sole defendant. Leaving a reported story aside for the moment, it should be added that the author of a signed contribution to a newspaper, in the form of an article or a letter, or even of a cartoon, is technically liable to an action for damages for libel. Indeed, one Dublin newspaper has cause to dearly remember a letter it published in recent years from a reader which contemptuously called into question the administration of justice after the hearing of a particular High Court case. Readers' letters are fraught with libel risks and should be carefully scrutinized. Care should also be exercised in publishing agency copy. The mere fact the wire services submit copy does not mean that the publishers are relieved of their obligations. The same can be said of re-publishing a story which has already appeared in another newspaper or has been televised or broadcast.

When the libel action comes to hearing, the various defendants are normally represented by a single set of counsel and firm of solicitors. It would be a sobering thought for all employees who could be named as defendants in a particular action to consider that the plaintiff could proceed against them to judgment were it not for the legal rule that makes their employer liable.

THE CASE FOR THE DEFENCE

Assuming that the plaintiff succeeds on the balance of probabilities in establishing that the words complained of referred to him, that the words were published to a third party and that they were defamatory or capable of being defamatory, it is then for the defence to consider its case. There are a number of legal defences open to the publishers. Success in any of them will defeat the plaintiff's claim.

The principal defences to an action for damages for libel are:
- justification
- privilege
- fair comment
- apology
- accord and satisfaction
- consent.

Of these, justification, privilege (absolute and qualified) and fair comment are the principal ones.

With regard to *justification*, it is a good defence to a civil action for libel that the words complained of are true in substance and in fact. But the proof required to establish such a plea is very strict, with the burden of proving it resting on the defendant. If the defendant fails to establish this plea, the consequence could be a sanction in the form of heavier damages for aggravating the libel.

With regard to *privilege*, if the words complained of are used either in the course of judicial or parliamentary proceedings or in the course of a fair and accurate report of judicial proceedings published contemporaneously there is absolute privilege, offering total immunity irrespective of ill-will or spite. This defence has the backing of the Constitution which, as far as reporting is concerned, states at Article 15.12:

> All official reports and publications of the Oireachtas or of either House thereof and utterances made in either House wherever published shall be privileged.

We shall deal with the matter more fully later under the heading 'Court Reporting' (see Chapter 3).

Qualified privilege is offered to certain newspaper and broadcast reports by section 24 of the Defamation Act, 1961 (see second schedule of 1961 Act). The one element which destroys privilege is *malice*. Malice, in law, is any wrong or improper motive, but it need hardly be added that malice is a stranger to the vocabulary of the working journalist.

The second schedule to the Defamation Act should be read and digested, but a word of explanation is necessary in order to fully understand what reports have qualified privilege.

Part I of the second schedule sets out four categories of reports which qualify for this privilege. They include reports from a house of the legislature of any foreign state; reports of an international organization or conference of which Ireland is a member or to which Ireland sends a representative; reports of an international court of justice or other tribunal deciding matters in dispute between states; court proceedings in foreign courts; and fair and accurate copies of extracts from a public registry. All of these are given qualified privilege *provided* they are fair and accurate and the proceedings to which the report relates were heard in public. However, the privilege attaches to proceedings in foreign courts even if they are not heard in public.

Part II of the second schedule sets out a long list of statements which are privileged 'subject to explanation or contradiction'. To understand the meaning of the words quoted above reference must be made to section 24(2) of the Defamation Act. Paraphrased, the sub-section states that these statements have qualified privilege only if it is proved in a libel action that the defendant has been requested by a defendant to publish in the newspaper or to broadcast from the broadcasting station from which the original broadcast was made a reasonable statement by way of explanation or contradiction, and has refused or neglected to do so, or has done so in a manner not adequate or not reasonable having regard to all the circumstances.

REPORT VERSUS COMMENT

Strictly speaking, only reports are privileged. It is, therefore, essential to distinguish between report and comment. A *report* is an account, abbreviated or otherwise, of proceedings. On the other hand, *comment* is the judgment or opinion of the journalist on these proceedings.

Whether journalists are engaged in reporting court or parliamentary proceedings, Bord Pleanála hearings, meetings of local authorities or any of the meetings or hearings given or deemed to be given qualified privilege in the second schedule of the 1961 Act, they should bear in mind the distinction between report and comment: if privilege is to be claimed in respect of fair and accurate reports, report and comment must be kept separate and distinct. No privilege can be claimed for comment, as distinct from strict reporting. Reporters should avoid editorializing: that is best left to the editorial writer.

Defending a libel action

FAIR COMMENT

Fair comment does not negative defamation but it establishes a defence to an action founded on defamation. The defence that the words complained of are a fair comment on a matter of public interest means that the words, although libellous, are not actionable.

Although it is primarily a matter for the newspaper's legal advisers to consider, both before and during the heat of a libel battle, journalists would do well to remember that comment may be no less damaging than strict reporting and that the law of libel does not allow a publisher and his journalistic employees unbridled expression of opinion. The matter commented upon must be of public interest and the comment must be acceptable to a fair-minded person.

THE PUBLIC'S RIGHT TO BE HEARD

One of the principles of natural justice affords journalists a beacon to follow in seeking to strike a sense of balance and fairness. That principle is *audi alteram partem* — the right to be heard. Lawyers speak of natural and constitutional justice in relation to the fairness of procedures which must be observed by tribunals, government ministers and others charged with the task of acting judicially. In recent years, the superior courts have condemned decisions which denied that fundamental right. Journalists, no less than public officials, are charged with the obligation of acting fairly. In no sense can a report be described as fair and balanced if the journalist choses to ignore the right of an individual to give his side of the story or to answer a claim made against him.

All too frequently, libel writs have been issued by individuals who were not contacted before the journalist went into print with an item of news or, worse still, a piece of gossip or hearsay taken on the word of a reliable source. Experience has taught that most often it is not the big exposé stories which have landed newspapers in hot water but the small, social-type items to which the same degree of care must be given as the 'hard news' story.

3

Court reporting

One of the greatest sources of danger as far as the law of libel is concerned is the court of law. In this country, there is an abundance of courts which provide newspapers, magazines, radio and TV with a plentiful supply of copy on a daily basis. The various courts are:

- The District Court — civil and criminal
- The Circuit Court — civil and criminal
- The High Court — civil
- The Central Criminal Court — criminal
- The Special Criminal Court — criminal
- The Court of Criminal Appeal — criminal
- The Supreme Court — civil but has jurisdiction to hear criminal appeals.

Add to these other types of hearings of a judicial nature such as, for example, Employment Appeal Tribunals and Army courts martial, to mention just two, and the source becomes even wider. By the very nature of court cases defamatory things will be said and reporting of them is only permissible because of the privilege accorded by the Defamation Act.

Section 18(1) of the Act states:

> A fair and accurate report published in any newspaper or broadcast by means of wireless telegraphy as part of any programme or service provided by means of a broadcasting station within the State or in Northern Ireland of proceedings publicly heard before any court established by law and exercising judicial authority within the State or in Northern Ireland shall, if published or broadcast contemporaneously with such proceedings, be privileged.

Section 18(2) states: 'Nothing in subsection (1) of this section shall authorise the publication or broadcasting of any blasphemous or obscene matter.'

Regarding subsection (1) three words, in particular, should be emphasised: 'fair', 'accurate' and 'contemporaneously'. To be given the mantle of privilege or immunity from suit, the report (not comment) of the case must be fair and accurate and the newspaper or other media branch must publish the report contemporaneously. This would seem to mean that the report should be published in the next available edition or bulletin.

'Publicly heard' in subsection (1) is also extremely important. Many reporters have experience of being present in court when the judge made an order to exclude the public or persons not directly concerned with the case. An example of this is to be found in section 16(2) of the Criminal Procedure Act, 1967. This states:

> Where the court is satisfied, because of the nature or circumstances of the case or otherwise in the interests of justice, that it is desirable, the court may exclude the public or any particular portion of the public or any particular person or persons except *bona fide* representatives of the Press from the court during the hearing.

The fact that the reporter is allowed to remain present and to fulfil his function would not, *per se*, limit his or her right to statutory privilege. However, if a judge, for a reason best known to himself or herself, rules that a certain case be held *in camera* and excludes the public, including the Press, from the hearing, the journalist who subsequently compiles a report by reference to the documents on file or in the possession of either party to the litigation or by getting an abbreviated version of the hearing from one or all of the parties, is treading on dangerous ground. Not alone would privilege not attach to such a report, but the reporter and the organ which published would face proceedings for contempt of court with fines, prison sentences and sequestration of assets as possible sanctions.

When a judge makes a ruling to hold a case *in camera* it must be obeyed. The matter is too grave for any one reporter to risk the ire of the bench for the sake of a story. However, occasions have arisen and, no doubt, will arise where such rulings have been questioned, but it must be done in a proper manner by legal representatives acting on behalf of the publisher, who will go before the judge in question or to a higher court on appeal to argue why the case should be heard in public. It may also be open to the legal representatives of the National Union of Journalists or such body representing journalists' interests to make similar submissions where public interest demands it. But these are legal questions and far outside the competence of journalists ultimately to decide.

A HEARING IN CHAMBERS

Occasionally a judge will decide to hear a case in chambers, that is, his or her own private office in the court building. No matter how important the case and regardless of the public interest, the reporter has no right of admission. The publication of a 'mish-mash' report of what occurs in chambers can lead to contempt proceedings. Reports of such private proceedings are not privileged.

A HEARING IN THE JUDGE'S HOME

Sometimes, because of the urgency of an issue such as where one party wants to apply *ex parte* to a judge of the High Court or Circuit Court for a temporary injunction against another party, it becomes necessary for a judge to hold the court in his or her own home. These situations are not uncommon but give rise to difficulty for a number of reasons. The party making the application may not readily cooperate with the inquiring journalist, and the judge in whose home the court is to be held may not be too anxious to allow reporters inside.

In approaching this problem, it must be stated that in the generality of cases judges are accommodating in this regard once the journalist acts reasonably. The occasion where the judge refuses access would be the exception.

Except in certain limited cases, justice 'shall' be administered in public, the Constitution states. The fact that the court is held in the judge's home is merely for the convenience of the party making the application. If the registrar attached to the court where the particular judge presides is known to the reporter, that person should be contacted as a matter of priority, to arrange attendance at the hearing. If the registrar's identity is not known or cannot be ascertained, the reporter's only recourse may be to go to the judge's home and seek admission directly.

WHEN IS A PRIVATE COURT HEARING NOT PRIVATE?

Apart from the occasions when the presiding judge allows the Press to remain in court to report proceedings while excluding the public and persons with no interest in the particular case, situations can arise where Press representatives find themselves in the invidious position of being allowed to stay and report extremely sensitive and delicate matters but only on terms laid down by the judge. One of the most important cases ever to be decided by the High Court fell within this category.

It involved an application under the Adoption Act which eventually led to changes in the adoption legislation. The reporters were forewarned that the natural parents of a young boy who had been adopted were about to apply to the High Court for an order directing the adoptive parents to return their son. When the court sat, counsel requested the judge to hold the proceedings *in camera*. The then existing adopion legislation gave no such power to the judge (although the judge had a discretion to hold it in private under the Censorship of

Publications Act, 1929 because an issue involving an infant was being considered), but he exercised his discretion in allowing the Press to remain and report the case to a conclusion by requesting, and getting, a commitment from the reporters not to publish anything about the case which would in any way permit identification of the parties, even the parts of the country where they resided.

The terms were strictly observed in the reporting and, when the case went on appeal, the Supreme Court allowed the appeal hearing to be reported on similar terms. However, some time after judgment was delivered, the court sat again on the case, only this time the Press were excluded under implied threat of contempt proceedings, even though the issue at the centre of the legal controversy had by then become a national issue with consequent Dáil debate and eventual new adoption legislation.

Similar restrictions apply to judgments in important family law cases such as where the grounds for obtaining an order for the nullity of a marriage are broadened as a result of a particular case. While the identity of the parties is preserved, publication is permitted, as a matter of practice, because of the public importance of the result.

THE CONSTITUTION

Article 34 of the Constitution expressly provides that:

> Justice shall be administered in courts established by law by judges appointed in the manner provided by this Constitution, and, save in such special and limited cases as may be prescribed by law, shall be administered in public.

Starting from the premise that the business of all courts should be conducted in public with the right to report automatically available, the Constitution gives the legislature power to de-limit that right where it considers it necessary. An obvious example is the Guardianship of Infants Act and other family law legislation where provision is built in to empower the court to hold hearings 'otherwise than in public'.

The reporter who transgresses the law in this respect and submits a story for publication will not be thanked for his or her initiative when the writs for contempt are served.

REPORTS OF JUDICIAL PROCEEDINGS

Before reporting a case are reporters free to extract information from files lodged in the central offices of the courts? These files contain copies of the pleadings, such as the Civil Bill and the Defence, the High Court Summons, the Statement of Claim, the Notice for Particulars, the Reply to the Notice, and the Defence, and possibly Affidavits. At District Court level, the Civil Process and possibly a Defence and Counterclaim are relevant in civil cases; in criminal cases the reporter may wish to see the summons or the charge sheet.

More often than not, the court clerk or Garda sergeant will make the documents available for perusal in the District Court on request, provided the request is reasonably made at a time which does not interfere with the running of the case; the registrars of the higher courts will also do so; but sometimes a journalist will 'get wind' of perhaps a controversial court case in advance of the date fixed for the hearing and may need to see the documents already on file. The question arises whether the journalist is entitled to see them and to extract information from them.

The only clear guideline available in this respect is the second schedule to the Defamation Act which refers to statements having qualified privilege. Among the six listed examples is one which may cover the journalist. It states:

> A fair and accurate copy of any extract from any register kept in pursuance of any law which is open to inspection by the public or any other document which is required by law to be open to inspection by the public.

It may be going too far to argue that the files in any of the central offices of the courts are open for public inspection; but, equally, it could be argued that they are. The question has never been tested in court, although one High Court judge some years ago directed an inquiry to be held after extracts from documents on file appeared in a Dublin newspaper prior to a particular hearing.

Courts administer justice evenly and it is incumbent on newspapers to report cases fairly and accurately. If the file contains only details of the plaintiff's claim and only this is published in advance of the hearing, the report hardly does justice to the defendant named in the suit. Journalists should, therefore, be on their guard to ensure that both parties to the dispute have their claims and denials reported fairly and accurately.

THE HEARING

Mere *ex parte* applications to a judge or justice may be fairly and accurately reported. Every step in every lawsuit taken in open court may be reported; in other words, a newspaper reporter may report everything that occurs publicly in open court without fear of being sued, provided the reports are fair and accurate and not interspersed with the reporter's comments.

Before proceeding further, it must be mentioned that there are limitations on the general right to report court proceedings.

As noted above, section 18(2) of the Defamation Act states:

> Nothing in subsection (1) of this section authorises the publication or broadcasting of any blasphemous or obscene matter.

Using the plain meaning of words, this means that blasphemous or obscene matter may not be published, even where it arises in court proceedings.

The second limitation is contained in the Censorship of Publications Act, 1929. All of the daily and evening newspapers operating in the State at the time have cause to remember this limitation from the reporting of one High Court divorce *a mensa et thoro* case in 1971.

Section 14 of the Act prohibits the printing or publishing of:

(a) indecent matter calculated to injure public morals;

(b) indecent medical, surgical or physiological details publication of which would be calculated to injure public morals;

(c) details of proceedings of judicial proceedings for divorce, nullity of marriage, judicial separation or restitution of conjugal rights, with certain exceptions.

The High Court reporters reported practically every detail of evidence tendered in the particular case which was heard in open court over a period of three or four days. There was no *in camera* sign on the door and no warning was given by the presiding judge. But some weeks later, summonses were served on all the newspapers alleging breaches of the 1929 Act in so far as evidence in the case was published. The 1929 Act lays down specific rules as to what can be published in such cases. Evidence is not included. The error was expensive. The District Court in Dublin fined each of the newspapers £200 for each breach i.e. each edition. The cost in fines alone to two of the newspapers was £1,200 each, which represented a hefty fine in 1971.

THE REPORT

When reporting a court case, the sworn evidence of the witnesses should be relied on rather than speeches of solicitor or counsel. All too frequently the opening speech is reported, particularly where the harassed reporter is working to evening paper deadlines or early broadcast bulletins. The reporter hurries away to telephone or fax the copy to the office without waiting to hear any evidence. If and when the reporter returns to the courtroom later, much of the evidence will have been given and the reporter is left to pick up the pieces and compile a report, either for later editions or for the daily newspaper of the following morning, from whatever is left of the day's hearing. It may even be that the case was settled while the court was bereft of reporters. Fairness and accuracy have been sacrificed in the interests of expediency.

Care should be taken to report the proceedings accurately and as fully as possible. The summing-up of the judge should also be reported. To be fair and accurate the report need not be *verbatim*. It may be abridged or condensed but it should not be lop-sided with undue emphasis on one side. Since the plaintiff is first in to bat in a civil case and the prosecution is first in in a criminal case, it is too easy to fall into the trap of over-emphasizing one side of the argument to the exclusion of the respondent or defendant. If a one-sided view of the case is published, this could, *prima facie*, constitute malice and leave the publisher without the defence of privilege.

THE 'PICK-UP'

One of the greatest pit-falls for newspapers is the court report picked-up by one reporter from another and sent over to the office without being checked. This situation has not been helped by the number of courts the reporter is directed to cover. Cut-backs by newspaper offices have resulted in fewer reporters being assigned on a regular basis to individual courts, particularly in urban areas, with the consequence that the reporter is directed or expected to pick-up a report from one or more courts.

At the best of times, publishing can be a risky business, but the news editor who so directs a reporter — either a member of the staff or a freelance — is inviting trouble. It is far better for a particular court case to go unreported than for a story to be picked-up latent with error. There have been several instances of this in recent times. One which readily comes to mind is where a Dublin newspaper paid out £3,000 libel damages to a man convicted of possessing drugs just because the reporter was not in court to see what transpired.

NAMES AND ADDRESSES

As with so many other facets of reporting, extreme care should be taken to ensure that the names and addresses of the respective parties to an action are transcribed accurately, in addition to particulars of the claim and defence (in civil proceedings) and of the charge (in criminal prosecutions). The only short-cut permissible is abbreviating details of the charge. With regard to names and addresses, giving the number of the house as stated in the official documents may often lead to problems. The party may have left the house and the new occupier may take exception to owning a property now in the full glare of publicity. Equally, a policy of not giving the number of the house can be troublesome where, for instance, there might be two or even more persons with the same name on the same road in towns or large urban areas. Indeed, provincial newspapers are particulaarly susceptible because of the proliferation of similar Christian and surnames in areas of the country, frequently in the same village.

However, once the name and address given in the court document are transcribed and published accurately, privilege should offer protection from suit. In the interests of complete accuracy and in fairness to the aggrieved party, the newspaper should, and usually does, publish a correction as soon as possible, even though the error is not of its making.

THIRD PARTIES

It may happen that reference is made in the course of a court hearing to something that is allegedly said by a person who is not in court or, indeed, that blame may be levied on such a third party, who does not have the opportunity to rebut the statement in court.

While the newspaper is protected with the immunity of privilege if it reports such statements accurately in an open court hearing, the editor is placed somewhat in a dilemna when the third party seeks redress by the publication of a disclaimer or apology. The newspaper is not a court of law to test the accuracy of the original statement or of the rebutting evidence of the third party. In such circumstances, the editor or, preferably, the newspaper's solicitors should advise the complainant to make a statement in open court, which then can be reported with the protection of privilege.

Unsupported allegations against people not present in court should not be over-emphasized either by the reporter filing the court report or by the sub-editor writing the heading on the copy.

HEADINGS

The sub-editor who writes the headings on court reports carries a heavy responsibility. With a tendency to sensationalize or to oversimplify, some newspapers have fallen into the trap of completely misrepresenting the storyline in court copy, with financial consequences to the proprietor and libellous publicity for a litigant.

DISTRICT COURT PRELIMINARY EXAMINATIONS

From time to time the reporting of preliminary examinations in the District Court has given rise to doubts on the part of reporters and their news editors as to what may or may not be published.

The answer is to be found in section 17(1) of the Criminal Procedure Act, 1967, which states:

> No person shall publish or cause to be published any information as to any particular examination other than a statement of the fact that such examination in relation to a named person on a specified charge has been held and of the decision thereon.

4

Contempt of court

DEFINITION

The essence of contempt of court is action or inaction amounting to interference with or obstruction to, or having a tendency to interfere with or to obstruct, the due administration of justice.

That definition from an old English case is cited by one of the main standard text books on criminal law, *Archbold*. An even shorter definition would be 'conduct offensive to a court of law or prejudicial to the course of justice'.

In the course of a lecture delivered at Queen's University, Belfast and published by the *Northern Ireland Legal Quarterly* in 1982, Mr Justice Seamus Henchy, then a Supreme Court judge and now Chairman of the Independent Radio and Television Commission, said that contempt of court, whether civil or criminal, whether committed in the face of the court or out of court, whether committed in relation to imminent, to pending, or to past proceedings, is a remedy aimed primarily, not at upholding the dignity of a court or a judge, but at enabling the administration of justice to operate without due obstruction or interference.

Civil contempt is a method of enforcing court orders and could hardly be said to affect journalists in the performance of their professional duties.

Criminal contempt represents the law's proscription as a crime of conduct deemed to be incompatible with the proper administration of justice.

A third category of contempt would be the publication of scandalous matter of the court itself. Criminal contempt and the third category are, therefore, those forms which affect journalists.

With regard to criminal contempt, when Kevin O'Kelly of RTE conducted an interview with Sean Mac Stíofáin it probably never crossed his mind that it might result in him being sent to prison. But it did, after refusing as a witness in the Special Criminal Court to identify the voice on the tape as that of Mr Mac Stíofáin (who was before the court charged with being a member of an illegal organization). The court sentenced the journalist to three months imprisonment for contempt, and he was duly conveyed to Mountjoy. However, he was not allowed to languish for long in prison. After being given bail pending the outcome of an expeditious appeal, Mr O'Kelly was fined £250 by the Court of Criminal Appeal, which upheld the conviction for contempt of court against him but varied the terms of the penalty to a fine instead of a prison sentence.

It is to be noted that the court did not commit Mr O'Kelly to prison for an indeterminate period or until he purged his contempt, as it was empowered to do. The case illustrates the fine balance that exists between the freedom of the journalist to disseminate a free flow of information, and the administration of justice.

When a case is pending which may ultimately be tried before a court, the common law rule is that nothing can be published which might interfere with the course of justice, even though the publication was due to a genuine mistake on the part of the reporter and was published in good faith with no intention to interfere with the course of justice. The court adjudicating on the contempt issue will seek to establish the *mens rea*, i.e. the mind of the reporter or publisher at the time of the breach, to determine the motive or otherwise.

The possibility of contempt of court proceedings lurks in every court. A simple bail application by an accused can, conceivably, lead to contempt proceedings if matter is published concerning the accused which might interfere with the accused's right to a fair trial. If, in the course of the bail application, a Garda witness testifies to the fact that he saw the accused rob a bank or discharge a firearm at pursuing members of the Force, publication of this evidence, even innocently, could prejudice the accused's subsequent trial before a jury. A court trying the contempt issue would adjudicate on the basis that the jurors might have read the newspaper report or heard the broadcast bulletin and so would have a preconceived idea about the guilt of the accused. When such breaches occur the accused's trial is normally adjourned for a long period to remedy, by the flux of time, whatever damage might have been caused.

A newspaper is also guilty of contempt of court if it refers to a previous conviction of the accused prior to the court or the jury having an opportunity to decide his guilt or innocence based on the evidence before them.

A 'prelim' report published about an accused in advance of the trial is also technically in contempt of court. In recent years there have been several instances of this, where criminal trials have had to be adjourned while the editor and, possibly, the publisher were called to task before the court.

And, as stated earlier, mistake or inadvertence does not excuse the breach. In one English case, the proprietors and editor of a newspaper were vicariously liable for the publication of a matter which might interfere with the course of justice even though the publication of such matter was due to a genuine mistake on the part of the reporter and was published in good faith with no intention to interfere with the course of justice.

The offence is committed if the publication is deemed likely to interfere with a fair trial. An Irish case decided that the power to attach for contempt may be exercised against a corporate body, i.e. the company which owned and/or published the newspaper.

Various pieces of legislation expressly give courts and tribunals power to deal with contempt issues. In Chapter 3, section 17(1) of the Criminal Procedure Act was referred to to illustrate the legislative prohibition on the publication of preliminary examinations in the District Court. Subsection (2) of the same section goes on to state:

> If it appears to a justice of the District Court, on the application of the Attorney General, that any person has contravened sub-

section (1), he may certify to that effect under his hand to the High Court and the Court may thereupon inquire into the alleged offence and after hearing any witnesses who may be produced against or on behalf of that person, and after hearing any statement that may be offered in defence, punish or take steps for the punishment of that person in the like manner as if he had been found guilty of contempt of the Court

The Act makes no reference to what form the punishment for contempt should take. One of the inherently unfair elements of the contempt laws where the media is concerned is the absence of specified fines and terms of imprisonment. The High Court has full discretion to impose a fixed but theoretically unlimited term of imprisonment or an unlimited fine. However, as with all decisions of the High Court, there is a right of appeal to the Supreme Court. No matter what court imposes the sanction after a finding of contempt, there always exists a right of appeal, the one exception being the Supreme Court, which is the final court of appeal.

PRESS PHOTOGRAPHERS AND CONTEMPT

Press photographers are frequently assigned to snap photographs of accused persons and witnesses as they enter and emerge from court buildings before, during and after trials. Does the publication of such photographs amount to contempt, particularly if they appear during the currency of the trial?

A very recent decision of the English Court of Appeal provides a helpful answer. A photographer from the Fleet Street tabloid, *The Sun,* together with colleagues from other newspapers, was interested in obtaining photographs of two men who were being tried for living on immoral earnings. When the two emerged from the court, *The Sun's* photographer started taking photographs, succeeding in the case of one of the accused; but the second accused put a newspaper over his head to prevent a close-up of his face being taken and the photographer followed him and persistently tried to take photographs despite it being made clear that the accused did not wish to be photographed. The incident ended when the accused bumped into scaffolding and possibly a lamp post and then made a dash for it with the photographer in pursuit. The photographer was found guilty of contempt of court. His conduct was held to amount an interference with the administration of justice and he was fined £500 and ordered to pay £500 costs. He appealed.

The Court of Appeal upheld the photographer's appeal. The Lord Chief Justice, Lord Lane, in the judgment, said the photographer's conduct was undoubtedly offensive, rude, uncivilized and wholly reprehensible but fell short of amounting to interference sufficient to constitute a contempt of court.

SCANDALIZING THE COURT

A Dublin newspaper published a statement in good faith which it had received from an organization. Like other newspaper offices, the particular office accepted the *bona fides* of the source of most statements received and duly published them. This statement seemed to be no different. But it was. The joint authors of the particular statement criticized the Special Criminal Court to such an extent that the Supreme Court, on appeal by the defendants from the High Court, ruled that they had scandalized the court and remitted the case to the High Court to allow the joint authors to be dealt with.

The situation that the newspaper found itself in — although its *bona fides* was accepted by the court — was little different from the other Dublin newspaper which published a letter from a reader in good faith but ended up in the dock for contempt. Both situations show that great care must be exercised where the letter or statement purports to reflect on the character, capacity or motives of an identified or identifiable person or, as we have seen, of a court.

COMMENT BY NEWSPAPERS ON COURT PROCEEDINGS

In summary then, although there is a right to publish a fair and accurate report contemporaneously with the court proceedings, no comment on them may be indulged in while the proceedings are still before the court. Comment is permissible only when the case is finally concluded and the decision is announced in a civil action or, in a criminal prosecution, by the conviction or acquittal of the defendant. The question might be asked whether it is possible to offer comment or to publish a follow-up story in relation to a decided civil action if the decision is going to be appealed. Under the rules governing the operation of the courts, a given period is allowed in which to lodge a notice of appeal — for example, a party to a High Court action is allowed 21 days. The considered view is that comment or a follow-up report would be permissible during that period, but as soon as the notice of appeal is lodged and this fact becomes publicly known, prudence would suggest that published comment should be avoided or at least restrained. There should be no expression of opinion, no colouring of a report, whether by emphasis or by omission, during the currency of a court hearing; newspapers, however, usually hold themselves free to comment on a case once it is concluded, even where the appeal notice has been lodged in the higher court. Each case must be viewed on its own circumstances. In one case involving an Irish magazine, where extended coverage had been given to a pending case, the judge hearing the contempt proceedings decided not to hold the publisher in contempt for the reason that such prior publicity could not be prejudicial since the case about which comment had been made was to be tried by a judge. A different view would probably have been taken were it to have come before a jury. Nonetheless, if an editor knows as a fact that proceedings are imminent or that an appeal is pending before any court, comment should be withheld until the case is finally determined. To act otherwise is to invite trouble. In the vast majority of cases nothing will happen, but it is better to err on the side of caution than to take the chance.

SUB JUDICE: LIMITS ON PUBLICATION

The *sub judice* rule has been a cause of much controversy over the years and a particular thorn in the side of news editors and investigative journalists. As explained earlier, a civil action is begun by issuing a summons or writ; a criminal prosecution by the issuing of a warrant or summons. Once this has been done, the proceedings are *sub judice* or pending, and no comment is permitted. In other words, once a question — civil or criminal — has passed into into the domain of the courts for judicial determination, any conduct calculated to interfere with the functions of the court could bring wrath, in the form of proceedings for criminal contempt, down on the heads of the violators. For a breach to have occurred, it would be necessary for the originating writ or summons to have been issued. An inquiring journalist is often met with a statement that a matter is *sub judice* because the issue in controversy has been handed to a solicitor or simply because a solicitor's letter has been sent on behalf of one party to another party in a particular dispute whereas in fact no originating writ or summons has been issued. In such circumstances, that issue would not be *sub judice*.

The rule would very much apply to situations where a suspect is brought before a District Court and charged with a criminal offence. Once the person is charged, nothing but the barest details may be published. These include the accused's name and address, details of the charge and the remand.

THE CONSTITUTIONAL GUARANTEE OF FREEDOM OF EXPRESSION

The Constitution guarantees the right of citizens to express freely their convictions and opinions but as with most rights this guarantee is not limitless. The fundamental rights portion of the Búnreacht, while expressing the right, states:

> The education of public opinion being, however, a matter of such grave import to the common good, the State shall endeavour to ensure that organs of public opinion, such as the radio, the press, the cinema, while preserving their rightful liberty of expression, including criticism of Government policy, shall not be used to undermine public order or morality or the authority of the State. . . .

Earlier, we have endeavoured to state the law as it is and has been applied by the Irish courts when the question of contempt arises in relation to comment on pending court proceedings and the *sub judice* rule. The parameters of the law are never fixed, and each new case that comes before the courts is capable of opening up new horizons and further loosening of the fetters that bind media comment. One such case, decided by the High Court in 1987, bears out much of what has been stated in this and the previous chapter; when editors are trying to make an on-the-spot decision as to whether they should publish or not, they may get some valuable help from the following comment by the judge in that High Court case:

> I do not see why a judgment cannot be criticised provided it is not done in a matter calculated to bring the Court or the judge into contempt. If that element is not present there is no reason why judgments should not be criticised. Nor does the criticism have to be confined to scholarly articles in legal journals. The mass media are entitled to have their say as well. The public takes a great interest in court cases and it is only natural that discussion should concentrate on the result of cases. So criticism which does not subvert justice should be allowed. . . .

5

Privacy

We all value our privacy and very often go to extreme lengths to protect it. As the saying goes: 'Love your neighbour but keep the fences up'. But what is the legal position regarding privacy — the state of being let alone, or freedom from human interference by any means, including the prying journalist?

Apart from the constitutional right to marital privacy which was read into the Constitution by the Supreme Court in 1972, there is no decision in this country which expressly recognizes the common law right to privacy. However, considerable protection is available to the public.

TRESPASS

The civil wrong of trespass gives generous protection of privacy interests: any wrongful entry onto property is actionable without the plaintiff having to prove that damage was caused. There is similar protection for trespass to a person's goods as well as trespass to the person.

NUISANCE

Nuisance is another actionable wrong and provides a head under which a person may sue in order to protect his privacy. An action taken in the English High Court about eleven years ago provides some assistance in considering the extent, at least, to which photographers may be permitted to photograph a person's private property.

In the particular case, an aerial photograph was shot of the plaintiff's residence, and the plaintiff, a lord of the realm, sued, but the court decided that the defendant was not liable in trespass because the plane had not flown unreasonably low over the property.

The judge, in delivering his decision, said he did not wish the judgment to be understood as deciding that in no circumstances could a successful action be brought against an aerial photographer to restrain his activities. He said:

> The present action is not founded in nuisance for no court would regard the taking of a single photograph as an actionable nuisance. But if the circumstances were such that a plaintiff was subjected to the harassment of constant surveillance of his home from the air, accompanied by the photographing of his every activity, I am far from saying that the court would not regard such a monstrous invasion of his privacy as an actionable nuisance for which they would give relief.

BREACH OF CONFIDENCE

Protection is also given by the law where there has been a breach of confidence by the disclosure of information which was confidentially obtained. *Irish Law of Torts* says that where contract is not relied upon, the plaintiff must establish three elements in his claim. First, the information must have 'the necessary quality about it', that is, it must not be something which is public property and public knowledge. Second, the information must have been imparted in circumstances importing an obligation of confidence. Third, there must be an unauthorized use of the information to the detriment of the party communicating it.

At the outset of this topic, mention was made of the Supreme Court case which gave life to the constitutional right to marital privacy. In that same case, one of the Supreme Court judges in the course of his judgment stated:

> Whilst the 'personal rights' [under the Constitution] are not

described specifically, it is scarcely to be doubted in our society that the right to privacy is universally recognised and accepted with possibly the rarest of exceptions. . . .

In 1972, the Committee on Privacy under the chairmanship of Lord Younger carried out a study and published a report on the protection of privacy.

In part, the committee said if there was to be a right of privacy under the law it should not, in their opinion, be synonymous with a right to be let alone. An unqualified right of this kind would in any event be an unrealistic concept, incompatible with the concept of society, which implies a willingness not to be let entirely alone and a recognition that other people may be interested and consequently concerned about us. If the concept were to be embodied into a right, its adaptation to the dominant pressures of life in society would require so many exceptions that it would lose all coherence and hence any valid meaning.

> We have concluded therefore that the type of conduct against which legal protection might be afforded on the ground of intrusion of privacy should be confined to injurious or annoying conduct deliberately aimed at a particular person or persons where the invasion of privacy in the principal wrong complained of.

The report went on:

> It is not contended in all the evidence to us that the information concerned [i.e. personal information] need be private, though if the information is also confidential its unauthorised handling is all the more objectionable. The unauthorised handling of informtion which may well be known or available through approved sources can also constitute a breach of privacy in certain circumstances. The most obvious example is where it is published at large to a far wider audience than would otherwise learn of it; the conduct of the mass information media is the main object of criticism under this heading.

The Younger Committee report said that placing someone in a false light was one of the four torts into which a particular author had analysed the United States law on privacy. The committee considered that placing someone in a false light was an aspect of defamation rather than privacy.

The committee stated that there was no legal right to privacy as such in the law of England and Wales, with at least one case in Scotland which suggested the opposite in that country.

The report continues:

> The laws of trespass to land and nuisance provide a right of action for invasion of privacy, if the victim is the legal occupier whose property is physically interfered with. But in the absence of actual damage, the remedy is an empty one....

The committee, with two dissentients, were against the introduction of a general right of privacy, despite the existence of such a right in some other common law jurisdictions.

In Britain, extra-legal protection of privacy may, to some extent be obtained through the activities of certain bodies including the Press Council, the BBC's Programme Complaints Commission and the Independent Broadcasting Authority's Complaints Review Board.

In this country, there is, as yet, no Press Council to which such complaints could be made and redress sought. However, there is a Broadcasting Complaints Commission which was established under the Broadcasting Authority (Amendment) Act, 1976, which is empowered by section 18 B to investigate and decide a range of complaints.

The Independent Radio and Television Act, 1988 which set up the Independent Radio and Television Commission has made no provision for the establishment of a similar complaints body, but there appears little doubt that once the new independent television and radio stations are up and running similar legislation will be enacted to deal with complaints from the public.

THE RIGHT TO BE LEFT ALONE

Although there is, as yet, no common law right of privacy, this country's Constitution ensures that the citizens are afforded certain fundamental protections although they are not expressly spelt out. That these include the personal right of privacy there can be no doubt. Mr Justice Liam Hamilton in the most recent High Court pronouncement on this right in 1987 preferred to call it 'the right to be left alone' and said:

> Though not specifically guaranteed by the Constitution, the right of privacy is one of the fundamental personal rights of the citizen which flows from the Christian and democratic nature of the State. It is not an unqualified right. Its exercise may be restricted by the constitutional right of others, by the requirements of the common good, and it is subject to the requirements of public order and morality.

There are many aspects to the right of privacy. Marital privacy is one that has been established by the Supreme Court. The recent action of the executive in 'tapping' the telephones of two journalists without any lawful authority, and in interfering with and intruding upon the privacy of the journalists in question, constituted an attack on their dignity and freedom as individuals and as journalists. It represents yet another aspect to the right of privacy, this time established by the High Court.

No doubt, as Mr Justice Hamilton stated in that case, the remaining aspects to the right to privacy will be dealt with when suitable cases come before the courts for determination.

6

Other topics

COPYRIGHT

Nothing will anger a journalist more than to see the fruits of his or her work 'lifted' and published in another newspaper or on radio or television without due acknowledgment. Such plagarism is not uncommon and leads to complaints of 'exclusive' reports in one newspaper being passed off as the work of journalists in another newspaper in subsequent editions. In strict law, the tort of passing off is committed where one trader represents his goods or services as those of another, so as to be likely to mislead the public and involve a considerable risk of detriment to the plaintiff; but, more properly, a journalist's work enjoys the protection of the law of copyright which in this country is governed by the Copyright Act, 1963.

Copyright is the exclusive right to print or otherwise multiply copies of a literary composition. Strictly there can be no copyright in the title of a newspaper. However, the courts, by injunction or damages, will protect the goodwill attaching to the exclusive use of a particular title. The law of copyright is a very specialized field and newspaper proprietors should, perhaps, consider taking particular legal advice in an effort to protect the work of their journalists as well as the reputation of their product and title.

THE OFFICIAL SECRETS ACT, 1963

No journalist in contemporary Irish society would give a minute's thought to the Official Secrets Act, believing that it is designed for the safeguarding of official information within the ambit of State servants with no relevance to the working journalist. But he or she would be wrong to make such an assumption.

While the Act *does* provide for the safeguarding of official information, journalists are, or should be, very much concerned with some of its provisions.

'Official information', within the meaning of the Act, means any secret official code word or password, and any sketch, plan, model, article, note, document or information which is secret or confidential or is expressed to be either and which is or has been in the possession, custody or control of a holder of a public office, or to which he has or had access, by virtue of his office, and includes information recorded by film or magnetic tape by any other recording medium.

'Official document' includes a passport, official pass, permit, document of identity, certificate, licence or other similar document, whether or not completed or issued for use, and also includes an endorsement thereon or addition thereto.

'Public office' is stated to mean an office or employment which is wholly remunerated out of the Central Fund or out of moneys provided by the Oireachtas, or an appointment to, or employment under, any commission, committee or tribunal set up by the Government or a Minister for the purpose of an inquiry, but does not include membership of either house of the Oireachtas.

The ambit of the Act and its powers are wide indeed when considered against the above definitions and give wide rein to the Government to institute prosecutions where its law officers consider that there has been a breach. In fact, considering the wide scope of the legislation, it would, perhaps, be surprising that so few prosecutions have been taken over the years, were it not for the fact that Ireland now enjoys a more open form of government with a better flow of information from official sources than was the case a quarter of a century ago.

Part II of the Act is the most relevant for journalists. This deals with the communication of information to the prejudice of the safety or preservation of the State. More specifically, section 9(1) states:

A person shall not, in any manner prejudicial to the safety or preservation of the State —

(a) obtain, record, communicate to any other person or publish, or
(b) have in his possession or under his control any document containing, or other record whatsoever of, information relating to —
   (i) the number, description, armament, equipment, disposition, movement or condition of any of the Defence Forces or of any of the vessels or aircraft belonging to the State,
   (ii) any operations or projected operations of any of the Defence Forces or of the Garda Síochána or of any of the vessels or aircraft belonging to the State,
   (iii) any measures for the defence or fortification of any place on behalf of the State,
   (iv) munitions of war, or
   (v) any other matter whatsoever information as to which would or might be prejudicial to the safety or preservation of the State.

The theft of a racehorse seems a most unlikely cause of a journalist, his editor and their newspaper proprietors being prosecuted under the Official Secrets Act, even when the horse's name is Shergar. But in 1983, in a rare prosecution under the Act, this occurred.

The owners of the Dublin newspaper published extracts from a *fógra* or notice circulated to Garda stations throughout the country which contained details of a number of persons Gardaí wanted to question in connection with the disappearance of the horse. Although the District Court acquitted the reporter in question, the editor and the newspaper owners were convicted.

SECTION 31

On 20 January 1977, the then Minister for Posts and Telegraphs by order brought into effect for twelve months section 31(1) of the Broadcasting Authority Act, 1960, which has been renewed by his successors every year since, most recently by the Minister for Communications in January, 1989.

Section 31(1) of the 1960 Act originally gave the Minister power to direct the RTE Authority in writing 'to refrain from broadcasting any particular matter or matter of any particular class'. The subsection made it mandatory on the Authority to comply with the Minister's direction.

When the Broadcasting Authority (Amendment) Act, 1976 was enacted, section 16 substituted the following subsection for subsection(1) of section 31:

> Where the Minister is of the opinion that the broadcasting of a particular matter or any matter of a particular class would be likely to promote, or incite to, crime or would tend to undermine the authority of the State, he may by order direct the Authority to refrain from broadcasting the matter or any matter of the particular class, and the Authority shall comply with the order.

The order which the RTE Authority is obliged to follow directs them to refrain from broadcasting any matter which is an interview, or report of an interview, with a spokesman or with spokesmen for any one or more of the following organisations, namely,

> (a) the organisation styling itself the Irish Republican Army (also the IRA and Óglaigh na hÉireann),

> (b) the organisation styling itself Provisional Sinn Féin,

> (c) any organisation which in Northern Ireland is a proscribed organisation within the meaning of section 28 of the Act of the British Parliament entitled the Northern Ireland (Emergency Provisions) Act, 1973.

Both section 31(1) and similar legislative restrictions introduced in

Britain and in Northern Ireland in 1988 are to be the subject of a legal challenge by broadcasting journalists, members of the National Union of Journalists, on the grounds, *inter alia*, that the provisions infringe freedom of speech and the dissimination of information.

BOOK PUBLISHERS

Although this handbook is designed for journalists, much of what it has to say will be of interest to publishers of books as distinct from newspapers and periodicals. Many journalists, moreover, are the authors of books; in that capacity they may be inclined to think that what is publishable in a newspaper, for example, is equally publishable in the text of a book. This is not the case for at least one important reason: books do not enjoy the protection of privilege which is given to *contemporaneous* reports of legal proceedings: thus, details of a case as reported, with privilege, in a newspaper cannot automatically be presumed to be publishable in a book which may appear even years later.

Many Irish book publishers have been surprised by a writ for libel and have incurred crippling settlement costs. The vast majority of book publishers, in this jurisdiction, are small businesses and have found it impossible to pay the large premiums involved in libel insurance — or, alternatively to 'carry their own insurance'. One effect of this state of affairs is that books by investigative journalists nowadays rarely see the light of day. Booksellers, too, are understandably conservative about which books they stock, because of their possible exposure to libel actions as distributors: whatever about a book publisher's familiarity with the detailed content of a book, a bookseller finds it impossible to keep track of it, and therefore — particularly in the case of the bigger bookshops — is inclined to play safe and not to stock books dealing with sensitive issues.

7

The National Union of Journalists

The vast majority of journalists working in the media in this country are members of the British-based National Union of Journalists, which introduced a Code of Professional Conduct in 1936. Apart from only one one amendment, the code has remained steadfast, as originally drafted, for more than fifty years.

The terms of the code are:

> 1. A journalist has a duty to maintain the highest professional and ethical standards.
>
> 2. A journalist shall at all times defend the principle of the freedom of the Press and other media in relation to the collection of information and the expression of comment and criticism. He/she shall strive to eliminate distortion, news suppression and censorship.
>
> 3. A journalist shall strive to ensure that the information he/she disseminates is fair and accurate, avoid the expression of comment and conjecture as established fact and falsification by distortion, selection or misrepresentation.
>
> 4. A journalist shall rectify promptly any harmful inaccuracies, ensure that correction and apologies receive due prominence and afford the right of reply to persons criticised when the issue is of sufficient importance.

5. A journalist shall obtain information, photographs and illustrations only by straightforward means. The use of other means can be justified only by over-riding considerations of the public interest. The journalist is entitled to exercise a personal conscientious objection to the use of such means.

6. Subject to justification by over-riding considerations of the public interest, a journalist shall do nothing which entails intrusion into private grief and distress.

7. A journalist shall protect confidential sources of information.

8. A journalist shall not accept bribes nor shall he/she allow other inducements to influence the performance of his/her professional duties.

9. A journalist shall not lend himself/herself to the distortion or suppression of the truth because of advertising or other considerations.

10. A journalist shall only mention a person's race, colour, creed, illegitimacy, marital status or lack of it, gender or sexual orientation if this information is strictly relevant. A journalist shall neither originate nor process material which encourages discrimination on any of the above-mentioned grounds.

11. A journalist shall not take private advantage of information gained in the course of his/her duties, before the information is public knowledge.

12. A journalist shall not by way of statement, voice or appearance endorse by advertisement any commercial product or service save for the promotion of his/her own work or of the medium by which he/she is employed.

Punishment by way of fine, suspension or expulsion is provided for in cases of 'conduct detrimental to the interests of the Union or of the profession'.

APPENDIX 1

The Defamation Act, 1961

AN ACT TO CONSOLIDATE WITH AMENDMENTS CERTAIN ENACTMENTS RELATING TO THE LAW OF DEFAMATION. [17*th August*, 1961.]

BE IT ENACTED BY THE OIREACHTAS AS FOLLOWS:—

PART I
PRELIMINARY AND GENERAL

1.—This Act may be cited as the Defamation Act, 1961.

2.—In this Act—

"local authority" has the same meaning as in the Local Government Act, 1941;

"newspaper", except in section 27, means any paper containing public news or observations thereon, or consisting wholly or mainly of advertisements, which is printed for sale and is published in the State or in Northern Ireland either periodically or in parts or numbers at intervals not exceeding thirty-six days;

"proprietor" means, as well as the sole proprietor of any newspaper, in the case of a divided proprietorship, the persons who, as partners or otherwise, represent or are responsible for any share or interest in the newspaper as between themselves and the persons in like manner representing or responsible for the other shares or interests therein, and no other person.

3.—(1) This Act shall come into operation on the 1st day of January, 1962.

(2) Part III of this Act shall apply for the purposes of any proceedings

begun after the commencement of this Act, whenever the cause of action arose, but shall not affect any proceedings commenced before the commencement of this Act.

4.—The enactments specified in the First Schedule to this Act are hereby repealed.

PART II
CRIMINAL PROCEEDINGS FOR LIBEL

5.—(1) On every trial of an indictment for making or publishing any libel to which a plea of not guilty is entered, the jury may give a general verdict of guilty or not guilty upon the whole matter put in issue on the indictment, and the jury shall not be required or directed by the court to find the person charged guilty merely on the proof of the publication by him of the paper charged to be a libel and of the sense ascribed to such paper in the indictment.

(2) On every such trial the court shall, according to its discretion, give its opinion and directions to the jury on the matter in issue in like manner as in other criminal cases.

(3) Subsections (1) and (2) of this section shall not operate to prevent the jury from finding a special verdict, in their discretion, as in other criminal cases.

6.—On the trial of any indictment for a defamatory libel, the person charged having pleaded such plea as hereinafter mentioned, the truth of the matters charged may be inquired into but shall not amount to a defence, unless it was for the public benefit that the said matters charged should be published; and, to entitle the defendant to give evidence of the truth of such matters charged as a defence to such indictment, it shall be necessary for the person charged, in pleading to the said indictment, to allege the truth of the said matters charged, in the manner required in pleading a justification to an action for defamation, and further to allege that it was for the public benefit that the said matters charged should be published, and the particular fact or facts by reason of which it was for the public benefit that the said matters charged should be published, to which plea the prosecutor shall be at liberty to reply generally, denying the whole thereof; and if, after such plea, the person charged is convicted on such indictment, the court may, in pronouncing sentence, consider whether his guilt is aggravated or mitigated by the said plea and by the evidence given to prove or to disprove the same: provided that—

(a) the truth of the matters charged in the alleged libel complained of by such indictment shall in no case be inquired into without such plea of justification;

(b) in addition to such plea of justification, the person charged may enter a plea of not guilty;

(c) nothing in this section shall take away or prejudice any defence under the plea of not guilty which it is competent to the person charged to make under such plea to any indictment for defamatory libel.

7.—Whenever, upon the trial of an indictment for the publication of a libel, a plea of not guilty having been entered, evidence is given establishing a presumption of publication against the person charged by the act of any other person by his authority, it shall be competent for the person charged to prove that the publication was made without his authority, consent or knowledge and that the publication did not arise from want of due care or caution on his part.

8.—No criminal prosecution shall be commenced against any proprietor, publisher, editor or any person responsible for the publication of a newspaper for any libel published therein without the order of a Judge of the High Court sitting *in camera* being first had and obtained, and every application for such order shall be made on notice to the person accused, who shall have an opportunity of being heard against the application.

9.—A Justice of the District Court, upon the hearing of a charge against a proprietor, publisher or editor or any person responsible for the publication of a newspaper for a libel published therein, may receive evidence as to the publication being for the public benefit, as to the matters charged in the libel being true, as to the report being fair and accurate and published without malice and as to any matter which, under this or any other Act or otherwise, might be given in evidence by way of defence by the person charged on his trial on indictment, and the Justice, if of opinion after hearing such evidence that there is a strong or probable presumption that the jury on the trial would acquit the person charged, may dismiss the case.

10.—If a Justice of the District Court, upon the hearing of a charge against a proprietor, publisher, editor or any person responsible for the publication of a newspaper for a libel published therein, is of opinion that, though the person charged is shown to have been guilty, the libel was of a trivial character and that the offence may be adequately punished by virtue of the powers conferred by this section, the Justice shall cause the charge to be reduced into writing and read to the person charged and shall then ask him if he desires to be tried by a jury or consents to the case being dealt with summarily, and, if such person consents to the case being dealt with summarily, may summarily convict him, and impose on him a fine not exceeding fifty pounds, and the Summary Jurisdiction Acts shall apply accordingly.

11.—Every person who maliciously publishes any defamatory libel shall, on conviction thereof on indictment, be liable to a fine not exceeding two hundred pounds or to imprisonment for a term not exceeding one year or to both such fine and imprisonment.

12.—Every person who maliciously publishes any defamatory libel, knowing the same to be false, shall, on conviction thereof on indictment, be liable to a fine not exceeding five hundred pounds or to imprisonment for a term not exceeding two years or to both such fine and imprisonment.

13.—(1) Every person who composes, prints or publishes any blasphemous or obscene libel shall, on conviction thereof on indictment, be liable to a fine not exceeding five hundred pounds or to imprisonment for a term not exceeding two years or to both such fine and imprisonment or to penal servitude for a term not exceeding seven years.

(2) (a) In every case in which a person is convicted of composing, printing or publishing a blasphemous libel, the court may make an order for the seizure and carrying away and detaining in safe custody, in such manner as shall be directed in the order, of all copies of the libel in the possession of such person or of any other person named in the order for his use, evidence upon oath having been previously given to the satisfaction of the court that copies of the said libel are in the possession of such other person for the use of the person convicted.

(b) Upon the making of an order under paragraph (a) of this subsection, any member of the Garda Síochána acting under such order may enter, if necessary by the use of force, and search for any copies of the said libel any building, house or other place belonging to the person convicted or to such other person named in the order and may seize and carry away and detain in the manner directed in such order all copies of the libel found therein.

(c) If, in any such case, the conviction is quashed on appeal, any copies of the libel seized under an order under paragraph (a) of this subsection shall be returned free of charge to the person or persons from whom they were seized.

(d) Where, in any such case, an appeal is not lodged or the conviction is confirmed on appeal, any copies of the libel seized under an order under paragraph (a) of this subsection shall, on the application of a member of the Garda Síochána to the court which made such order, be disposed of in such manner as such court may direct.

PART III
Civil Proceedings for Defamation

14.—(1) In this Part—

"broadcast" has the same meaning as in the Wireless Telegraphy Act, 1926 (in this section referred to as the Act of 1926) and "broadcasting" shall be construed accordingly;

"broadcasting station" has the same meaning as in the Act of 1926, as amended by the Broadcasting Authority Act, 1960;

"wireless telegraphy" has the same meaning as in the Act of 1926.

(2) Any reference in this Part to words shall be construed as including a reference to visual images, gestures and other methods of signifying meaning.

(3) Where words broadcast by means of wireless telegraphy are simultaneously transmitted by telegraph as defined by the Telegraph Act, 1863, in accordance with a licence granted by the Minister for Posts and Telegraphs, the provisions of this Part shall apply as if the transmission were broadcasting by means of wireless telegraphy.

15.—For the purposes of the law of libel and slander the broadcasting of words by means of wireless telegraphy shall be treated as publication in permanent form.

16.—Words spoken and published which impute unchastity or adultery to any woman or girl shall not require special damage to render them actionable.

17.—In any action for defamation, it shall be lawful for the defendant (after notice in writing of his intention so to do, duly given to the plaintiff at the time of filing or delivering the plea in the action) to give in evidence, in mitigation of damage, that he made or offered an apology to the plaintiff for such defamation before the commencement of the action, or as soon afterwards as he had an opportunity of doing so, in case the action shall have been commenced before there was an opportunity of making or offering such apology.

18.—(1) A fair and accurate report published in any newspaper or broadcast by means of wireless telegraphy as part of any programme or service provided by means of a broadcasting station within the State or in Northern Ireland of proceedings publicly heard before any court established by law and exercising judicial authority within the State or in Northern Ireland shall, if published or broadcast contemporaneously with such proceedings, be privileged.

(2) Nothing in subsection (1) of this section shall authorise the publication or broadcasting of any blasphemous or obscene matter.

19.—In an action for slander in respect of words calculated to disparage the plaintiff in any office, profession, calling, trade or business held or carried on by him at the time of the publication, it shall not be necessary to allege or prove special damage, whether or not the words are spoken of the plaintiff in the way of his office, profession, calling, trade or business.

20.—(1) In an action for slander of title, slander of goods or other malicious falsehood, it shall not be necessary to allege or prove special damage—

    (a) if the words upon which the action is founded are calculated to cause pecuniary damage to the plaintiff and are published in writing or other permanent form; or

    (b) if the said words are calculated to cause pecuniary damage to the plaintiff in respect of any office, profession, calling, trade or business held or carried on by him at the time of the publication.

(2) Section 15 of this Act shall apply for the purposes of subsection (1) of this section as it applies for the purposes of the law of libel and slander.

21.—(1) A person who has published words alleged to be defamatory of another person may, if he claims that the words were published by him innocently in relation to that other person, make an offer of amends under this section, and in any such case—

- (a) if the offer is accepted by the party aggrieved and is duly performed, no proceedings for libel or slander shall be taken or continued by that party against the person making the offer in respect of the publication in question (but without prejudice to any cause of action against any other person jointly responsible for that publication);

- (b) if the offer is not accepted by the party aggrieved, then, except as otherwise provided by this section, it shall be a defence, in any proceedings by him for libel or slander against the person making the offer in respect of the publication in question, to prove that the words complained of were published by the defendant innocently in relation to the plaintiff and that the offer was made as soon as practicable after the defendant received notice that they were or might be defamatory of the plaintiff, and has not been withdrawn.

(2) An offer of amends under this section must be expressed to be made for the purposes of this section, and must be accompanied by an affidavit specifying the facts relied upon by the person making it to show that the words in question were published by him innocently in relation to the party aggrieved; and for the purposes of a defence under paragraph (b) of subsection (1) of this section no evidence, other than evidence of facts specified in the affidavit, shall be admissible on behalf of that person to prove that the words were so published.

(3) An offer of amends under this section shall be understood to mean an offer—

- (a) in any case, to publish or join in the publication of a suitable correction of the words complained of, and a sufficient apology to the party aggrieved in respect of those words;

(b) where copies of a document or record containing the said words have been distributed by or with the knowledge of the person making the offer, to take such steps as are reasonably practicable on his part for notifying persons to whom copies have been so distributed that the words are alleged to be defamatory of the party aggrieved.

(4) Where an offer of amends under this section is accepted by the party aggrieved—

(a) any question as to the steps to be taken in fulfilment of the offer as so accepted shall, in default of agreement betwee the parties, be referred to and determined by the High Court or, if proceedings in respect of the publication in question have been taken in the Circuit Court, by the Circuit Court, and the decision of such Court thereon shall be final;

(b) the power of the court to make orders as to costs in proceedings by the party aggrieved against the person making the offer in respect of the publication in question, or in proceedings in respect of the offer under paragraph (a) of this subsection, shall include power to order the payment by the person making the offer to the party aggrieved of costs on an indemnity basis and any expenses reasonably incurred or to be incurred by that party in consequence of the publication in question;

and if no such proceedings as aforesaid are taken, the High Court may, upon application made by the party aggrieved, make any such order for the payment of such costs and expenses as aforesaid as could be made in such proceedings.

(5) For the purposes of this section words shall be treated as published by one person (in this subsection referred to as the publisher) innocently in relation to another person if, and only if, the following conditions are satisfied, that is to say—

(a) that the publisher did not intend to publish them of and concerning that other person, and did not know of circumstances by virtue of which they might be understood to refer to him; or

(b) that the words were not defamatory on the face of them, and the publisher did not know of circumstances by virtue of which they might be understood to be defamatory of that other person,

and in either case that the publisher exercised all reasonable care in relation to the publication; and any reference in this subsection to the publisher shall be construed as including a reference to any servant or agent of the publisher who was concerned with the contents of the publication.

(6) Paragraph (b) of subsection (1) of this section shall not apply where the party aggrieved proves that he has suffered special damage.

(7) Paragraph (b) of subsection (1) of this section shall not apply in relation to the publication by any person of words of which he is not the author unless he proves that the words were written by the author without malice.

22.—In an action for libel or slander in respect of words containing two or more distinct charges against the plaintiff, a defence of justification shall not fail by reason only that the truth of every charge is not proved, if the words not proved to be true do not materially injure the plaintiff's reputation having regard to the truth of the remaining charges.

23.—In an action for libel or slander in respect of words consisting partly of allegations of fact and partly of expression of opinion, a defence of fair comment shall not fail by reason only that the truth of every allegation of fact is not proved, if the expression of opinion is fair comment having regard to such of the facts alleged or referred to in the words complained of as are proved.

24.—(1) Subject to the provisions of this section, the publication in a newspaper or the broadcasting by means of wireless telegraphy as part of any programme or service provided by means of a broadcasting station within the State or in Northern Ireland of any such report or other matter as is mentioned in the Second Schedule to this Act shall be privileged unless the publication or broadcasting is proved to be made with malice.

(2) In an action for libel in respect of the publication or broadcasting of any such report or matter as is mentioned in Part II of the Second Schedule to this Act, the provisions of this section shall not be a defence if it is proved that the defendant has been requested by the plaintiff to publish in the newspaper in which the original publication was made or to broadcast from the broadcasting station from which the original broadcast was made, whichever is the case, a reasonable statement by way of explanation or contra-

diction, and has refused or neglected to do so, or has done so in a manner not adequate or not reasonable having regard to all the circumstances.

(3) Nothing in this section shall be construed as protecting the publication or broadcasting of any matter the publication or broadcasting of which is prohibited by law, or of any matter which is not of public concern and the publication or broadcasting of which is not for the public benefit.

(4) Nothing in this section shall be construed as limiting or abridging any privilege subsisting (otherwise than by virtue of section 4 of the Law of Libel Amendment Act, 1888) immediately before the commencement of this Act.

25.—An agreement for indemnifying any person against civil liability for libel in respect of the publication of any matter shall not be unlawful unless at the time of the publication that person knows that the matter is defamatory, and does not reasonably believe there is a good defence to any action brought upon it.

26.—In any action for libel or slander the defendant may give evidence in mitigation of damages that the plaintiff has recovered damages, or has brought actions for damages, for libel or slander in respect of the publication of words to the same effect as the words on which the action is founded, or has received or agreed to receive compensation in respect of any such publication.

27.—(1) The proprietor of every newspaper having a place of business in the State shall, where such proprietor is not a company registered under the Companies Acts, 1908 to 1959, and is not required under the provisions of the Registration of Business Names Act, 1916, to be registered under that Act in respect of the business of carrying on such newspaper, be registered in the manner directed by that Act, and that Act shall apply to such proprietor in like manner as it applies to a firm or individual referred to in section 1 thereof.

(2) Every reference in the Registration of Business Names Act, 1916, to that Act shall be construed as a reference to that Act as extended by subsection (1) of this section.

(3) In this section "newspaper" means any paper containing public news or observations thereon, or consisting wholly or mainly of advertisements, which is printed for sale and is published in the State either periodically or

in parts or numbers at intervals not exceeding twenty-six days.

28.—Nothing in this Part shall affect the law relating to criminal libel.

FIRST SCHEDULE
ENACTMENTS REPEALED

PART I
Acts of the Parliament of Ireland

Session and Chapter	Title
28 Hen. 8, c. 7 (Ir.).	An Act of Slaunder.
2 Geo. 1, c. 20 (Ir.).	An Act to limit the time for Criminal Prosecutions for words spoken.
33 Geo. 3, c. 43 (Ir.).	An Act to remove doubts respecting the functions of juries in cases of libel.

PART II
Acts of the Parliament of the late United Kingdom of Great Britain and Ireland

Session and Chapter	Title
60 Geo. 3 & 1 Geo. 4, c. 8.	Criminal Libel Act, 1819.
3 & 4 Vic., c. 9.	Parliamentary Papers Act, 1840.
6 & 7 Vic., c. 96.	Libel Act, 1843.
8 & 9 Vic., c. 75.	Libel Act, 1845.
32 & 33 Vic., c. 24.	Newspapers Printers and Reading Rooms Repeal Act, 1869.
44 & 45 Vic., c. 60.	Newspaper Libel and Registration Act, 1881.
51 & 52 Vic., c. 64.	Law of Libel Amendment Act, 1888.
54 & 55 Vic., c. 51.	Slander of Women Act, 1891.

SECOND SCHEDULE
STATEMENTS HAVING QUALIFIED PRIVILEGE

PART I
Statements privileged without Explanation or Contradiction

1. A fair and accurate report of any proceedings in public of a house of any legislature (including subordinate or federal legislatures) of any foreign sovereign State or any body which is part of such legislature or any body duly appointed by or under the legislature or executive of such State to hold a public inquiry on a matter of public importance.

2. A fair and accurate report of any proceedings in public of an international organization of which the State or the Government is a member or of any international conference to which the Government sends a representative.

3. A fair and accurate report of any proceedings in public of the International Court of Justice and any other judicial or arbitral tribunal deciding matters in dispute between States.

4. A fair and accurate report of any proceedings before a court (including a courtmartial) exercising jurisdiction under the law of any legislature (including subordinate or federal legislatures) of any foreign sovereign State.

5. A fair and accurate copy of or extract from any register kept in pursuance of any law which is open to inspection by the public or of any other document which is required by law to be open to inspection by the public.

6. Any notice or advertisement published by or on the authority of any court in the State or in Northern Ireland or any Judge or officer of such a court.

PART II
Statements privileged subject to Explanation or Contradiction

1. A fair and accurate report of the findings or decision of any of the following associations, whether formed in the State or Northern Ireland, or of any committee or governing body thereof, that is to say:

(a) an association for the purpose of promoting or encouraging the exercise of or interest in any art, science, religion or learning, and empowered by its constitution to exercise control over or adjudicate upon matters of interest or concern to the association or the actions or conduct of any persons subject to such control or adjudication;

(b) an association for the purpose of promoting or safeguarding the interests of any trade, business, industry or profession or of the persons carrying on or engaged in any trade, business, industry or profession and empowered by its constitution to exercise control over or adjudicate upon matters connected with the trade, business, industry or profession or the actions or conduct of those persons;

(c) an association for the purpose of promoting or safeguarding the interests of any game, sport or pastime, to the playing or exercise of which members of the public are invited or admitted, and empowered by its constitution to exercise control over or adjudicate upon persons connected with or taking part in the game, sport or pastime;

being a finding or decision relating to a person who is a member of or is subject by virtue of any contract to the control of the association.

2. A fair and accurate report of the proceedings at any public meeting held in the State or Northern Ireland, being a meeting *bona fide* and lawfully held for a lawful purpose and for the furtherance or discussion of any matter of public concern whether the admission to the meeting is general or restricted.

3. A fair and accurate report of the proceedings at any meeting or sitting of—

(a) any local authority, or committee of a local authority or local authorities, and any corresponding authority, or committee thereof, in Northern Ireland;

(b) any Judge or Justice acting otherwise than as a court exercising judicial authority and any corresponding person so acting in Northern Ireland;

(c) any commission, tribunal, committee or person appointed, whether in the State or Northern Ireland, for the purposes of any inquiry under statutory authority;

(d) any person appointed by a local authority to hold a local inquiry in pursuance of an Act of the Oireachtas and any person appointed by a corresponding authority in Northern Ireland to hold a local inquiry in pursuance of statutory authority;

(e) any other tribunal, board, committee or body constituted by or under, and exercising functions under, statutory authority, whether in the State or Northern Ireland;

not being a meeting or sitting admission to which is not allowed to representatives of the press and other members of the public.

4. A fair and accurate report of the proceedings at a general meeting, whether in the State or Northern Ireland, of any company or association constituted, registered or certified by or under statutory authority or incorporated by charter, not being, in the case of a company in the State, a private company within the meaning of the Companies Acts, 1908 to 1959, or, in the case of a company in Northern Ireland, a private company within the meaning of the statutes relating to companies for the time being in force therein.

5. A copy or fair and accurate report or summary of any notice or other matter issued for the information of the public by or on behalf of any Government department, local authority or the Commissioner of the Garda Síochána or by or on behalf of a corresponding department, authority or officer in Northern Ireland.

APPENDIX 2

A guide to legal terms
for the assistance of journalists

Accessory before the fact A person who assists in the commission of a crime by advice or cooperation before the crime is committed.

Accessory after the fact A person who, knowing that a crime has been committed, assists the criminal to escape from justice.

Accord and satisfaction An established defence in actions, e.g. libel and slander, the essence of which is that the plaintiff has previously agreed to withdraw his action on certain conditions and that the defendant, upon such an undertaking, has fulfilled these conditions.

Actus reus The guilty act in a crime.

Affidavit A sworn statement in writing.

Aggravated damages An increased measure of damages given by a judge or jury where the conduct of the defendant has been so wanton and reckless as to injure the plaintiff to an exceptional degree.

Appeal An application to a higher court to revise a decision of an inferior court or tribunal.

Appeal, Court of Criminal A court composed of three superior court judges — one from the Supreme Court and two from the High Court — which sits in the Four Courts, Dublin and hears appeals from the Circuit Criminal Court, the Special Criminal Court and the Central Criminal Court. It is also empowered by legislation to refer points of law of 'exceptional public importance' to the Supreme Court for determination.

Appellant A person or other entity such as a corporate body at whose instance an appeal is taken.

Arson The malicious setting fire to a dwelling house or certain other kinds of property.

Attorney General The chief legal adviser to the Government.

Attorney, power of A written authority given by one person to another to act legally in his name.

Bail Money deposited or pledged to ensure a person's appearance before a court.

Bailee A person with whom property is pledged or deposited, e.g. a pawnbroker.

Blasphemy The offence of reviling or ridiculing the accepted tenets of religion. An element of criminal libel.

Brief The written instructions prepared by solicitors for barristers conducting cases before courts or tribunals.

Certiorari A writ ordering the removal of a trial from one court to another, e.g. from an inferior to a higher court.

Case Stated A statement of facts prepared by a court in order to get the opinion of a higher court on a point of law.

Central Criminal Court The criminal arm of the High Court.

Contempt of Court Conduct offensive to a court or prejudicial to the administration of justice.

Copyright The exclusive right to make copies of an original work.

Counsel Barristers, including Senior Counsel, and members of the Junior Bar.

Criminal libel A libel so grave or so dangerous a character, that it is the fit subject of criminal proceedings.

Damages, general Such damages as the law presumes to have resulted from a civil wrong (a tort) without the plaintiff having to prove special injury.

Damages, special Direct loss and damage as the plaintiff can prove he suffered as a result of the defendant's wrongful conduct.

Defamation The publication of words injurious to another person's character or reputation.

Discovery A legal proceeding in the Circuit Court or High Court by which a party to a civil action is ordered to disclose on oath any documents in his possession or procurement bearing on the issue in dispute.

Exemplary damages The awarding of damages that are so heavy as to make an example of a defendant.

Ex-parte proceedings Proceedings conducted on behalf of one party to a civil action in the absence of the other.

Fair comment Just and reasonable comment on matters of public interest.

Felony A term applied to some serious forms of crime which attract a prison sentence.

Habeas corpus An order by the High Court directing a person such as a prison authority or a Garda Síochána to bring a prisoner before the court to justify the grounds of his or her detention.

Injunction An order of a civil court (excluding the District Court) commanding the performance of or the prohibition of some act, disobedience to which is punishable as contempt of court.

Innuendo The interpretation placed by the plaintiff on words which are the subject of an action for damages for libel.

Intra vires Within the power of.

Justification A defence to an action for damages for libel which obliges the plaintiff to prove the truth of the libel.

Libel A permanent representation such as writing the effect of which is to injure a person's good name by holding him up to public ridicule, hatred or contempt.

Mandamus A writ issued by a higher to a lower court ordering it to perform some duty.

Misdemeanour A less serious form of crime which does not amount to a felony.

Notary public An officer of the court, usually a solicitor in practice, authorized to certify deeds, contracts, affidavits and other legal documents.

Onus of proof The burden of proof is the obligation to prove a set of facts by evidence. In a civil action, the plaintiff must prove his case on the balance of probabilities; in a criminal prosecution, the prosecution must prove the accused's guilt beyond a reasonable doubt.

Plaintiff The party who brings the complaint in a civil action.

Pleadings The documents exchanged between the parties to a civil action during the preparation of the case for trial.

Prima facie On a first view; a *prima facie* case is one which raises a presumption of the accused's guilt sufficient that he or she be sent forward for trial.

Privilege A special legal right or immunity.

Punitive damages Damages so heavy as to punish a defendant in a civil action whose conduct has been of a flagrant nature and a gross infringement of the plaintiff's right.

Recognizances An undertaking given to a court to do or not to do a particular act, e.g. to appear at a future date, or to be of good behaviour for a stated period. Breach of the undertaking can lead to forfeiture of a certain sum.

Sine Die A Latin phrase meaning 'without a day'. It is used when legal proceedings are adjourned indefinitely. The term is normally associated with inquests at the Coroner's Court.

Slander Defamatory words uttered by word of mouth.

Solicitor A lawyer who conducts general legal business, manages law suits and instructs counsel in the superior courts.

Specific performance A legal remedy granted against a defendant which directs him to perform a contract in the plaintiff's favour.

Sub judice The term applied when legal proceedings have been commenced, any public comment on which is contempt of court.

Subpoena A summons addressed to a witness ordering his attendance in court for the hearing of an action.

Surety A person who goes bail for another.

Ultra vires A Latin phrase meaning outside or beyond the power, applied e.g. when a local authority exceeds its legal powers or a court or tribunal its jurisdiction.

Without prejudice The phrase used in relation to a letter written or an admission made in the course of negotiations, on the understanding that it will not be used against the party making it in the event of an action at law.